FEMALE ACTIVISTS

WOMEN
IN THE
WORLD™

FEMALE
ACTIVISTS

LENA KOYA AND ALEXANDRA HANSON-HARDING

Rosen
YA™

New York

Published in 2018 by The Rosen Publishing Group, Inc.
29 East 21st Street, New York, NY 10010

Copyright © 2018 by The Rosen Publishing Group, Inc.

First Edition

Library of Congress Cataloging-in-Publication Data

Names: Koya, Lena, author. | Hanson-Harding, Alexandra, author.
Title: Female activists / Lena Koya and Alexandra Hanson-Harding.
Description: New York: Rosen Publishing, 2018 | Series: Women in the world
| Audience: Grades 7–12. | Includes bibliographical references and index.
Identifiers: LCCN 2017016772 | ISBN 9781508177203 (library bound) | ISBN
9781508178835 (paperback)
Subjects: LCSH: Women—Political activity—Juvenile literature. | Women social
reformers—Juvenile literature. | Women's rights—Juvenile literature.
Classification: LCC HQ1236 .K69 2017 | DDC 305.42—dc23
LC record available at https://lccn.loc.gov/2017016772

Manufactured in the United States of America

CONTENTS

Female activists have been making history for as long as history has been recorded. Boudicca was an inspirational political and military leader of several British tribes in the first century. She successfully led her army to victories in search of independent rule for her people. In the fifth century, Hypatia of Alexandria was a well-known mathematician, astronomer, and philosopher. But there are also accounts of her speaking out for women's rights, particularly for basing one's judgment of women not on physical characteristics but on mental fortitude.

In modern times, too, many women have fought for their rights and the rights of others—and changed the world in the process. Women such as Sojourner Truth were instrumental in the US abolitionist movement to end slavery. They also fought for their right to vote in the early twentieth century, as well as in the civil rights movement to end segregation and race-based discrimination fifty years later. Some of the names of these influential

Malala Yousafzai is a well-known activist for women's and children's rights and the youngest-ever Nobel Prize laureate.

7

women are well known—including Susan B. Anthony, Elizabeth Cady Stanton, Rosa Parks, and Alice Walker. Others, including Septima Poinsette Clark and Fannie Lou Hamer, are perhaps less well known. But their fame matters less, in the end, than their accomplishments. These women worked tirelessly—and, oftentimes, thanklessly—to change the course of history and provide rights for entire groups of people around the world.

Women are continuing to fight in the struggle for increased rights for all people today. Young Pakistani activist Malala Yousafzai, in particular, has motivated millions in her fight for women's education and basic human rights. After surviving an attempt on her life, Yousafzai's voice has not been silenced. In 2014, she was awarded the Nobel Peace Prize for her efforts. She is the youngest-ever laureate for this prestigious prize.

These women chose to speak out against intolerance and injustice, despite the risks they faced along the way. Many of these famous activists lived relatively normal lives before deciding to dedicate their lives to activism. Today, girls and young women from all walks of life can heed their call to help others too. They can dedicate a few minutes to helping a neighbor or classmate, or they can get deeply involved in a particular cause to which they can dedicate their entire lives. Either way, they can make a difference. Just taking a stand against injustice when you see it can be a powerful force and propel young women into activism.

Many young women today are choosing to dedicate their lives in some way to bettering the world—and it is one of the most important things they can do in their lives. As Nicholas Kristof and Sheryl WuDunn wrote in their groundbreaking book *Half the Sky: Turning Oppression into Opportunity for Women Worldwide,* "The tide of history is turning women from beasts of burden ... into full-fledged human beings ... The question is ... whether each of us will be part of that historical movement, or a bystander."

CHAPTER 1

WOMEN AND ACTIVISM

Dr. Amy Lehman was on vacation in sub-Saharan Africa when she discovered her life's mission. While visiting Lake Tanganyika in eastern Africa, she discovered how few health care resources were available for those people who lived in the remote areas around the lake. The area has struggled with civil unrest over the past two years and is home to several of the world's poorest countries. So, with a small team of helpers, Lehman decided to take action. She began to deliver malaria nets to people living in the small lakeside villages. These lifesaving nets prevent people from being bitten by infected mosquitoes while they sleep.

That's not all. Lehman decided to raise funds to buy and set up a specially equipped hospital ship to help even more people. The goal

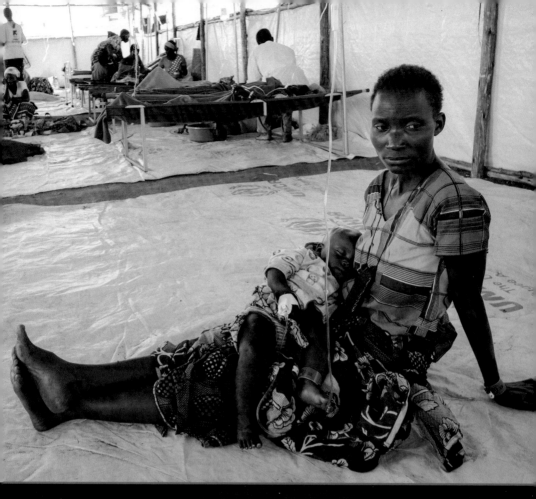

Amy Lehman's Lake Tanganyika Floating Health Clinic helps many people around Lake Tanganyika in eastern Africa who would not otherwise have access to health care.

of the ship was to bring high-level hospital care to people in remote villages without roads, electricity, or running water. "If you decide that you are going to do something that's trailblazing, you're stuck," she told the *Daily Beast*. "You have to have your steeled guts." The Lake Tanganyika Floating Health Clinic has already helped improve the lives of 450,000 people. Her determination shows what a tough woman can do when she puts her mind to it. But her accomplishments are built upon the work of other strong women throughout history.

FEMALE ACTIVISTS AND ABOLITIONISM

In Seneca Falls, New York, in July 1848, Elizabeth Cady Stanton spoke before a mixed assembly of women and men. She was angry at the injustices that women faced in America at that time. For example, married women could not own property—including their own wages, inheritances, or even the clothes on their backs. If they left their marriages, they had no rights to see their children. Some people at the time were trying to make the case that women were valuable because they were the "angels of the hearth," who inspired men to be finer. But when they tried to make men finer, women's efforts were not always welcomed.

At that time, another struggle for human rights was emerging—the struggle to end slavery, called the abolitionist movement. Many women were becoming prominent leaders in this movement. Angelina and Sarah Grimké were two daughters of a slave-owning family from Charleston, South Carolina. They began to lecture—shockingly, before mixed audiences of men and women! They became the first women lecturers of

Activist Sarah Grimké worked together with her sister Angelina to end slavery and grant women broader rights in the United States.

the American Anti-Slavery Society. When some men complained that they were not being ladylike, Sarah Grimké wrote a book called *Letters on the Equality of the Sexes and the Condition of Woman* (1838), which contained a groundbreaking defense of the right of women to speak in front of men and women. Grimké wrote, "I ask no favors for my sex ... All I ask of our brethren is that they will take their feet from off our necks, and permit us to stand upright on the ground which God has designed us to occupy."

Stanton fought for the abolitionist cause, too. She also thought it was wrong for women to be second-class citizens, going beyond what Grimké demanded. At the Seneca Falls Convention on Women's Rights, she laid down a fiery proposition. She said that women deserved the same rights men had—including the right to vote—not because of their moral superiority, but because they were human beings, no better or worse than men. They deserved education, the chance to own their own money, and everything else that gave men their privileged place. She declared that women had the right to be free and protected from laws that, at that time, gave a man the right to take his wife's wages, the property she inherited, and in the case of divorce, her children.

In a famous speech in September 1848, Stanton said, "In carrying out his own selfishness, man has greatly improved woman's moral nature, but by an almost total shipwreck of his own ... We would not have woman less pure, but we would have man more so. We would have the same code of morals for both."

She believed that these laws depriving women of rights could not be changed until women had suffrage, or the right to vote. After the Civil War, the slaves were freed and black males had the legal right to vote (though that right was often quashed by racist laws in the South). But despite the efforts of various women leaders, women's suffrage would not be achieved for many years.

ABOLITIONIST AND SUFFRAGETTE: SOJOURNER TRUTH

Sojourner Truth was born into slavery in upstate New York in approximately 1797. In her late twenties, she escaped with her infant daughter to freedom. However, she was forced to leave her young son behind. Truth stayed with a family of abolitionists for a year until the New York State Emancipation Act was signed in 1827. Soon after, she discovered that

(continued on page 17)

Sojourner Truth escaped slavery to become a well-known lecturer, abolitionist, and women's rights activist.

(continued from page 15)

her five-year-old son has been sold to a slave owner in Alabama. Truth sued her former owner for having illegally sold her son and won the court case. She reunited with her son in 1828.

In 1843, Truth set off on a lecture series around the United States for the abolitionist cause. She would go on to become a famous and valued speaker for abolitionism. Her most famous speech, "Ain't I a Woman?," was delivered at the Women's Convention in Akron, Ohio, on May 29, 1851. This speech, delivered to a crowd of suffragettes, encouraged white women and black women to work together for both universal suffrage and the abolition of slavery. The speech famously begins:

> "That man over there says that women need to be helped into carriages, and lifted over ditches, and to have the best place everywhere. Nobody ever helps me into carriages, or over mud puddles, or gives me any best place! And ain't I a woman? Look at me! Look at my arm! I have ploughed and planted, and gathered into barns, and no man could head me! And ain't I a woman?"

TWENTIETH-CENTURY FEMALE ACTIVISTS

The suffragists' determination finally had an effect. The Nineteenth Amendment to the US Constitution, giving women the right to vote, was ratified in 1920.

During World War II, with many men at war, women entered the workforce in growing numbers. They built planes and warships, and they were praised for their contributions. Heroic pictures of a mythical female worker named Rosie the Riveter were everywhere. But when the war ended and soldiers returned home, employers laid off women workers by the thousands. Instead, they were encouraged to be stay-at-home housewives.

During the 1960s, a new rebellion against the stifling roles of women grew. Betty Friedan wrote *The Feminine Mystique* in 1963, objecting to these restrictions. In 1966, she became the first president of the National Organization for Women (NOW).

During the early 1970s, the post–World War II economic boom ended. Jobs were becoming less secure. Having two incomes became increasingly necessary for many families. Women went back to work, creating two-wage households. Women made many professional advances as the women's liberation movement took off. From that time to today, women have continued to move forward. But the struggle for equality continues.

HONORING WOMEN'S HISTORY

We can honor these past women whose bravery changed life for girls and women today by honoring women's history. The following are some projects to pursue in order to draw greater attention to women's activism historically:

- **Support a museum dedicated to women's history.** Meryl Streep has played many roles in her acting career. But one of her most important life roles is working to open a new museum celebrating women's history in Washington, DC. Why is this effort so important to her? As she told *Vogue* magazine, "Because our history was written by the other team, basically." Teens can help make the National Women's History Museum become real by donating money to the project, displaying the museum's badge online to alert Facebook friends, or blogging about the museum. To learn more, check out the National Women's History Museum's website (http://www.nwhm.org).
- **Curate a women's history exhibit.** Teens can also keep women's history alive by using space in their school to make a women's history exhibit. To learn how, go to a museum and study how information is displayed. Then learn about female role models,

Actress Meryl Streep has been a vocal supporter of the National Women's History Museum to showcase the important contributions women have made.

either local or national. Find photos and artifacts, and write captions to tell their story. Ask if you can use a display case in your school to show them off.

- **Record it.** Use a video camera to interview older people about their lives. Visit a nursing home, or speak with elderly relatives and neighbors. Make a list of questions beforehand about how life has changed for women since they were young. Take time to listen if the conversation goes in an unexpected direction. Share the interviews with your classmates.

- **Aid the floating clinic.** Help Amy Lehman's Lake Tanganyika Floating Health Clinic through donations or fundraising activities. For more details, check out the clinic's website (http://www.floatingclinic.org).

CHAPTER 2

WOMEN IN THE MEDIA

It's easy to see the differences in how women and men are represented in the media. Female actresses typically display the Hollywood ideal of long legs and narrow waists. Their appearances are often judged before their intelligence or talents. Take the Academy Awards, for example. When celebrity reporters interview female celebrities, they are often first asked about the dress and jewelry they are wearing, instead of their Academy Award-nominated performances. Conversely, men are more often asked about their roles, their inspiration, and their dedication to their jobs. While these might seem like trivial differences, media representations of women that focus entirely on their appearances—above all else—have very real consequences.

Actresses Kristin Chenoweth (*left*) and Jessica Chastain (*right*) speak on the red carpet of the Academy Awards. Actresses are often judged more for their appearances than their talent.

POSITIVE ROLE MODELS

It can be hard for young girls to find positive role models for themselves in the media. Oftentimes, depictions of women and girls are based on stereotypes, such as the social climber, the trophy wife, or the soccer mom. Some of the most famous cartoons for young girls feature girls as princesses, such as Princess Jasmine or Snow White. This can be unhelpful to girls because, in reality, the role of princess is basically a passive one—a princess is really just the daughter of a king and, oftentimes, her only goal is to find her prince. While recent Disney princesses, including Merida from *Brave* and Elsa from *Frozen*, challenge these stereotypes, there is still much more that can be done to create better role models for young girls.

Meanwhile, boys star in TV shows more frequently than girls do, and they are shown in a wider variety of roles. In 2008, a study by the International Central Institute for Youth and Educational Television looked at about twenty thousand children's programs in twenty-four countries. The research showed that girls only made up 32 percent of the shows' main characters.

SELLING AN IMAGE

Often, advertisements sell more than a product. They sell an image. A lot of advertising works at an

Princess Merida from the Disney film *Brave* is one of the few role models for girls who challenges media stereotypes of women.

unconscious level. It makes girls worry. Is their hair shiny enough? Are their hands soft? Do they have thunder thighs? Ragged nails? Limp hair? "Cankles"? What about their figures? Advertisers invent new "problems" that make women feel as if they are unworthy—unless they buy their products.

According to a 2010 report from the American Psychological Association (APA), culture's emphasis on beauty and sex appeal can increase girls' vulnerability to depression, distorted body image, and eating disorders. In one study of teen girls, for instance, girls with a tendency toward self-objectification— judging their body in terms of how beautiful and desirable they think it looks to others—were more likely to experience depression and had lower self-esteem.

Dissatisfaction with their bodies may lead teen girls to seek plastic surgery. As author Peggy Orenstein notes, cosmetic surgery is a multimillion-dollar business in the United States. According to the American Society of Plastic Surgeons (ASPS), 63,623 cosmetic surgeries were performed on teenagers in 2013. Most of these elective surgeries consisted of nose reshaping, ear pinning, or breast augmentations.

AIRBRUSHED REALITY

Ironically, nobody looks as good as the models in magazines—not even the models themselves.

The media's fixation on beauty and sex appeal can increase girls' vulnerability to distorted body image and eating disorders.

Advertisers use computer programs to airbrush the images of models and stars into perfection. Airbrushing distorts photos. It takes away blemishes, pinches in waists, and lengthens legs. Some advertisers even alter images to put one model's head on another model's body.

Dr. Hany Farid and doctoral student Eric Kee from Dartmouth College invented a computer program that analyzed 468 sets of unedited and airbrushed photos of models. Each changed photograph was judged on a scale of one to five, with images rated five showing the heaviest retouchings. Farid and Kee have spoken out about the need for a universal health warning to be put on airbrushed magazine images to show teens that what they see is not real.

CELEBRITIES AGAINST AIRBRUSHING

Some celebrities are taking a stand against airbrushing as well. In 2015, when actress Kate Winslet signed on to renew her contract as a spokeswoman for beauty brand Lancôme, she required that all of her photos be "free of any additional editing."

(continued on page 30)

Actress Kerry Washington has spoken out publicly against magazines that have airbrushed her image without her permission and the harm that unrealistic images can cause.

(continued from page 28)

Explaining her decision not to allow her image to be airbrushed, Winslet noted how magazines influenced teenage girls:

> I think they do look at magazines, I think they do look to women who have been successful in their chosen careers and they want people to look up to, and I would always want to be telling the truth about who I am to that generation because they've got to have strong leaders. We're all responsible for raising strong young women, so these are things that are important to me.

Other celebrities have also taken action against unrealistic media depictions, including Helen Mirren, Zendaya, and Kerry Washington. Kerry Washington has called out magazines for seemingly airbrushing her skin to make it look lighter, a form of editing that is often used with celebrity women of color. In response to an apology issued by *InStyle* for a cover photo of Washington that made her skin color appear much lighter, she wrote: "Thank [you for] opening this [conversation]. It's an important [one] that needs to be had." Washington and others have spoken publicly about the need for African-American teen girls to have role models who look like them depicted in the media.

TURNING WOMEN INTO OBJECTS

There are many ways that women are stereotyped. But one of the most damaging stereotypes for young girls is showing women as sex objects. Ads like these can be found in almost every magazine and on almost every television channel. For example, an ad campaign for People for the Ethical Treatment of Animals (PETA) wasn't so ethical when it came to using sexist images of women. One ad showed a naked model lying in a pile of strategically placed chili peppers with the caption "Spice Up Your Life." Another ad featured actress Pamela Anderson in a skimpy bikini with marks all over her body listing her body parts. The ad reads, "All animals have the same parts." These ads are certainly attention getting—but they also turn women into objects.

OTHER REPRESENTATIONS

According to the Screen Actors Guild, only about 38 percent of acting roles go to women. Most of those roles are as sidekicks and girlfriends. Some movies portray strong women, such as the crusading Erin Brockovich, the brave young heroine of *Winter's Bone,* or the athletes of *A League of Their Own.* But most movies that star women are "chick flicks" featuring the message that a woman needs to find romance with a man to be happy. Some examples are *Twilight, Austenland,* and *Sleepless in Seattle.*

Even news reporters are not immune to the pressure to be young, beautiful, and thin. Many times they are young and dressed in glamorous clothes—reporting the news next to men who are often much older and face less pressure to be judged on their appearance.

FIGHTING FOR FAIR MEDIA IMAGES

Teens can start by examining the kinds of images that exist in the media and identifying the messages they send about women. Then, they can use their power to change destructive images and combat their effects. Here are some ways to get involved:

- **Start a media club.** Ask a teacher to sponsor a school club to examine media and how it portrays women. Gather evidence and share it. Ask, how does media, including advertising, try to manipulate people? Have members bring in different kinds of magazines and newspapers and study the ads. What are they saying? For example, some ads literally turn women into objects (such as a vodka bottle). Teens can also talk about movies you've seen, from comedies to action movies. What do the women look like? Are the heroines much younger than the heroes? Two great websites to use as resources to start discussions are Media Smarts (http://www.mediasmarts.ca), and About Face (http://www.about-face.org).

- **Make a YouTube video mash-up.** Teens can take their examination of images a step further. Use a phone or video camera to create a mash-up of sexist images from advertisements and magazines. Learn statistics about advertising and add comments in between images. Then post the video on YouTube.

- **Raise your voice.** Teens who find objectionable ads can write about them on a blog, comment on other blogs, or write to the company. If an offensive advertisement appears during a show you like, write to the network to say that you find the advertisement inappropriate. Write reviews for your school or local paper about how women are being affected by sexist media.

- **Boycott.** If women's magazines, celebrity websites, or TV shows set up unrealistic ideals for women, stay away from them. Don't buy those magazines or even visit those websites online.

- **Spend smart.** Buy products that support positive images of girls and women.

Actress Jennifer Lawrence plays a strong heroine, named Katniss Everdeen, in the Hunger Games films. Lawrence's character is one of very few powerful female protagonists.

- **Make a "vision board."** Teens can collect and share positive images of girls from magazines, newspapers, articles, or their own drawings or photographs. Get a large piece of posterboard and put them together to create a "vision board" of these positive images. Display them in homeroom or in the hallways. Teens can also write positive letters to ad makers who make positive ads.
- **Have a film festival.** In spite of the negative stereotypes or weak images often seen on TV shows or in movies, some have powerful women

main characters. Share ideas about good shows, movies, and videos. Then share movies that have positive roles for women. Examples include *Moana, Hunger Games, Whale Rider, A League of Their Own, Mona Lisa Smile,* and more.

- **Go on a media diet.** Think about how the media tries to shape teens' moods. Go on a media diet. Each spring, the Campaign for a Commercial-Free Childhood sponsors Screen-Free Week. It recommends that the week be a time to "unplug and play, read, daydream, create, explore, and spend time with family and friends." Teens can get their own schools involved. Work with teachers to think of prizes and activities to encourage participation. The organization offers materials to help leaders organize activities for the week at http://www.screenfree.org.

- **Take it further.** Teens can cut their screen time year-round. Take back your sense of reality from the world of media. Clean out your head. Put quality knowledge, literature, and information in there instead. Do something that will give you confidence. The more you focus on real life, the less you'll be affected by the messages around you.

CHAPTER 3

IMAGE, ABILITY, AND HEALTH

Many teens around the world are obsessed with their weight. This is due, in part, to the media messages being sent to them about an ideal body type, as well as the judgment often passed on women's physical characteristics rather than on their abilities. Unfortunately, this has led to a proliferation of eating disorders such as anorexia nervosa and bulimia nervosa, particularly in North America. According to the National Association of Anorexia Nervosa and Associated Disorders (ANAD), nearly thirty million people suffer from an eating disorder in the United States. About 1 percent of all

Eating disorders affect all races and ethnic groups. According to the National Association of Anorexia Nervosa and Associated Disorders (ANAD), about 1 percent of American women will suffer from anorexia in their lifetime.

37

female adolescents suffer from anorexia and about 4 percent of college-aged women suffer from bulimia. While anorexics starve themselves even if they are extremely thin, bulimics eat but then purge the food they eat in order to lose weight. These conditions can lead to kidney failure and even death. And yet, at the same time, according to the Centers for Disease Control and Prevention (CDC), approximately one in five school-aged children (from six to nineteen) are obese. Since 1980, the number of obese youth has almost tripled.

TEENS AND DISORDERED EATING

Most people know that eating a double cheeseburger and fries with a giant soda or eating a whole tub of ice cream is unhealthy. But lots of teenagers do it anyway. This can leave them feeling sick and bloated— or worse, put them in danger of metabolic syndrome. That includes heart problems, high blood pressure, diabetes, and other disorders. Once a teen becomes obese, taking the weight off can be difficult.

Restaurants are serving larger and larger portions. Inexpensive, fatty food is available everywhere, and it is tempting to fill up with a cheap and quick meal. Living in "food deserts"—mostly rural or urban areas where affordable, quality, healthy food is difficult to get—makes healthy diets harder. And of course, advertisements have a way of making the unhealthiest foods look completely irresistible. On the cover of women's magazines, pictures of gorgeously decorated cupcakes jostle with images of super-skinny models and lines about how to lose that extra 10 pounds (4.5 kilograms) of belly fat. Readers get mixed messages in magazines, on television, and through other media. This can give girls an artificial relationship with their hunger. Instead of eating healthy foods in response to their natural appetites, many girls end up constantly craving less nutritious treats.

According to the Huffington Post, there is a $60 billion diet industry in the United States. There are also dangerous "pro-ana" groups where anorexics gather online to talk about how to lose even more weight. Both obesity and anorexia are serious health problems that show a lack of balance about food. Doctors call this disordered eating.

WOMEN AND SPORTS

In her famous 1848 address, Elizabeth Cady Stanton said, "We cannot say what the woman might be physically, if the girl were allowed all the freedom of the boy in romping, climbing, playing whoop and ball." At that time, women received exercise mainly through work, in fields, in factories, and at home. Meanwhile, they wore restrictive clothes, such as tight corsets that

Runner Paula Radcliffe set the fastest women's marathon time in 2003. Just twenty years earlier, women weren't allowed to run in marathons at all.

pinched in their waists and huge skirts with petticoats. Not until the 1890s could women enjoy a sport for fun, according to Sue Macy, author of *Wheels of Change: How Women Rode the Bicycle to Freedom (With a Few Flat Tires Along the Way)*. Macy reports that in 1896, when women started joining the new bicycling craze, women's rights' pioneer Susan B. Anthony said that bicycling "has done more to emancipate women than anything else in the world." Suddenly, women got to go outside unsupervised. They got to wear more practical clothes. And they got to enjoy moving for pleasure.

According to the US Department of Health and Human Services, teens need sixty minutes of exercise a day for good health. Unfortunately, only 27 percent of teens are actually getting that amount. Why? One reason may be that, according to a Kaiser Family Foundation study, eight- to eighteen-year-olds in the United States spend an average of seven and a half hours a day on "screen time" alone. That's more than fifty-three hours a week! Yet, physical activity brings a number of benefits. Not only does it help build strong muscles and healthy bones, it improves mood.

Ironically, though many teen girls aren't moving enough, this is a time when more girls are getting involved in athletics than ever before. Once, few sports were open to girls at school. Then, in 1972, Title IX of the Education Amendments was passed. This law

Olympian Katie Ledecky is one of the fastest swimmers in the world—male or female.

gave girls the same resources as boys in athletic and academic programs funded by the federal government. Title IX increased girls' access to sports dramatically. According to the Feminist Majority Foundation, today more than 40 percent of all college and high school athletes are female.

Until the 1980s, women weren't allowed to run the 26.2-mile marathon. Now, women run marathons by the thousands, and the fastest woman's time of 2:15:25, set by Paula Radcliffe in 2003, is a mere thirteen minutes slower than Dennis Kimetto's record of 2:02:57, set in 2014. Women are catching up in other sports as well.

Jockey Julie Krone, for instance, faced fierce competition from the best male jockeys of her day, but during her long career in horse racing, she had 3,545 victories. She also had more than $81 million in lifetime earnings, according to ABC Sports Online. In 2010, she became the first female jockey to be entered into the National Thoroughbred Racing Hall of Fame.

Swimmer Katie Ledecky has often been compared to male swimmers due to her speed and strength despite her desire to be taken as an athlete in her own right and not based on her gender. In 2016, right before Ledecky won four gold medals and one silver medal at the Rio Olympics, swimmer Ryan Lochte famously said of Ledecky, "This girl is doing respectable times for guys." According to ESPN journalist Kavitha A. Davidson, comments such as these are "a vestige of still seeing sports as [an] inherently male space, and of mostly male fans and commentators unable or unwilling to consider female athletes by their merits alone."

SEXUAL HEALTH

Another important aspect of teens' health is their sexuality. When teens don't understand the facts about how their bodies work and how to protect themselves, they can make dangerous choices. According to the CDC, 41 percent of high school students had sexual intercourse in 2015. Its statistics also show that nearly ten million fifteen- to twenty-four-year-olds get sexually transmitted diseases in the United States each year. That may be, in part, because 43 percent did not use a condom the last time they had sex.

The human papilloma virus (HPV) is a virus that can cause cervical cancer as well as genital warts through sexual contact. A vaccine called Gardasil can be given both to boys and girls. It can prevent HPV. But it works best if given before a young person has had sexual contact.

The deadliest sexually transmitted disease is HIV/AIDS. In 2015, young people age thirteen to twenty-nine made up 22 percent of all new HIV cases, according to the CDC. Condoms can help cut the spread of this disease. So can abstinence, or refraining from having intercourse. Right now, HIV can be controlled but not cured.

The United States also has the highest teen pregnancy rate in the industrialized world. According to the CDC, in 2015, nearly 230,000 fifteen- to nineteen-year-old girls gave birth. Only half of teen mothers earn high school diplomas by age twenty-two, as opposed to 90 percent of girls who haven't given birth. Teen mothers face many economic and social challenges.

EMBRACING A POSITIVE BODY IMAGE

Teens can help themselves—and each other—develop a healthy relationship with their bodies. The following ideas can help teen girls develop a positive body image and live healthier lives:

- **Become friends with food.** Ironically, the best way to get a healthy, less obsessive relationship with food is to be mindful and pay attention to it—in a new way. Teens should focus on nourishing themselves instead of starving themselves or feeling guilty. The US Department of Agriculture's Choose My Plate program

Teens can learn the importance of eating a healthy diet in part by growing vegetables themselves.

(http://www.choosemyplate .gov) is a good place to start learning about nutrition. The program recommends that you fill half your plate with vegetables and fruits at every meal. The site even has a food tracker to help you keep track of what you eat and learn more about nutrition. If you start to eat better, your body will start to feel better. In addition, learning how to cook healthy, appealing food is a powerful act of independence. As food writer Michael Pollan says, if you want a simple guide to healthy eating: "Eat food. Not too much. Mostly plants."

- **Grow a healthy food culture.** Teens may feel more ownership of vegetables if they see them growing. At Northern Valley Regional High School in Old Tappan, New Jersey, students have a garden that includes everything from herbs to tomatoes. To start a garden, it's important to plan well. You will need to locate a sunny, somewhat enclosed area with an easily available source of water. Work with a teacher to get permission from the school, and ask for donations from local businesses for soil, seeds, and fertilizer. Get other students to commit to planning and growing the garden. Then, plant away! For more advice, check out http://www.kiwimagonline .com/2013/06/building-a-garden.

- **Fight eating disorders.** Learn the signs of eating disorders. People with anorexia, for instance, starve themselves because of an irrational fear of becoming fat. Physical symptoms of anorexia (aside from extreme thinness) include dry skin, growth of body hair on arms and legs, weakness, and cold hands and feet. Anorexics often exercise compulsively, are secretive about their eating habits, and are obsessed with calories. To learn more, one good resource is the National Eating Disorders Association (NEDA). You can help the organization by joining walks to raise funds and awareness. Often, these walks take place during National Eating Disorders Awareness Week (usually held in late February). The National Association of Anorexia Nervosa and Associated Disorders (ANAD) is another helpful organization.

- **Move it!** Teens can find an exercise they like and move. Even better, they can get moving with a friend! Shoot some hoops, dance, or try jogging. Bike short distances instead of driving to do errands. Even if you are just hanging out at home or talking on the phone, stand up and walk whenever you can. You can do it all at once or in short chunks, even ten minutes at a time, to reach a sixty-minute goal. By starting now, you can develop a lifelong exercise habit.

- **Count to ten thousand.** Another way of getting healthy is to take ten thousand steps a day. There are many devices that you can use to count your steps, from a simple pedometer, to a fitness watch, to phone apps. You can count your steps walking around school, walking from the parking lot to the store, etc. If you are uncomfortable setting a goal of ten thousand steps to begin with, try building up to it by adding five hundred steps to your goal each week. Keep a log of your progress and feel proud when you meet your goals.

- **Love yourself.** Being positive about your body can be one of the best motivators for taking care of it. Check out the NOW Foundation's Love Your Body campaign (http://now.org/now-foundation /love-your-body). Another positive site, Operation Beautiful, was started by Caitlin Boyle, who started leaving positive messages on Post-it notes for other girls and women to find. See http:// operationbeautiful.com.

- **Get excited about women's sports**. Go to a women's basketball game or other women's sports event at a local college. Be a booster for a girls' team at your school. Unfortunately, these great athletes don't always get the attention—and attendance—they deserve. Showing up and rooting for them sends a powerful message.

- **Think carefully about sex.** Choosing to engage in sexual behavior is a serious decision and teens should understand its potential consequences. Ask a doctor or family member, or learn from such trusted sites such as Planned Parenthood (http://www.plannedparenthood.org/info-for-teens) or the CDC (http://www.cdc.gov/TeenPregnancy/index.htm). Never act just to please a partner—everyone has the right to wait until he or she is ready. Many teens may find that they want to wait before taking on the adult responsibilities that come with sex.

MYTHS AND
FACTS

There are many misconceptions regarding the health and physical abilities of women. Here are a few such misconceptions with the facts that refute these claims:

MYTH: Women's sports can't compete with men's sports.

FACT: Women have made great strides in professional sports. In fact, women's records in swimming and track and field have shown greater improvements than men's records.

MYTH: You can tell if someone has an eating disorder just by looking at them.

FACT: You cannot know if someone has an eating disorder just based on their weight alone. People with eating disorders come in different shapes and sizes and may not appear drastically underweight or overweight.

MYTH: Only women get eating disorders.

FACT: Approximately one out of every ten people with an eating disorder is male. Eating disorders also disproportionately affect transgender individuals. Approximately 16 percent of trans individuals state that they have been diagnosed with an eating disorder over the past year.

CHAPTER 4

FIGHTING FOR WOMEN— AND AGAINST VIOLENCE

In *Dreamland*, a popular YA novel by Sarah Dessen, sixteen-year-old Caitlin O'Koren finds herself drawn to the rich and spoiled but brilliant Rogerson Biscoe. As they become closer, however, Biscoe becomes more and more controlling. He watches O'Koren's every movement and wants to know where she is at all times. Then he begins hitting her. Even though her parents and friends are understanding in most situations, O'Koren is so ashamed that she finds herself unwilling to tell them. She puts up with increasingly dangerous behavior and then doesn't know how to get out

Actress Gabrielle Union was appointed under President Barack Obama to work on a White House committee addressing how to prevent violence against women.

of the relationship as the violence escalates. This kind of cruel behavior, called dating violence, is just one of the four types of violence that will be explored in this chapter. According to the National Coalition Against Domestic Violence (NCADV), one in four women and one in seven men have been the victims of violence by an intimate partner in their lifetimes.

DATING VIOLENCE

Dating violence is an abusive relationship pattern in which one partner uses physical or emotional threats to control the other. In dating violence, one partner may start with put-downs that make the victim feel less confident. The abuser may stalk the victim or order her not to go places without his consent. He may start punishing her mentally or physically, with threats, hair pulling, kicks, or other violent acts.

DOMESTIC VIOLENCE

Domestic violence is similar to dating violence but usually occurs in situations in which partners are married or live together or have recently separated. According to a report from the Senate Judiciary Committee, domestic violence is the number-one cause of injury to women between the ages of fifteen and forty-four. Women between the ages of eighteen and twenty-four are the most commonly abused by partners.

A Ford Foundation study found that half of the homeless women and children in the United States were fleeing from abusers. For many women, leaving an attacker may involve losing homes, jobs, and money—or even their lives. According to the Center for American Progress, of all the female

Men and women have to work together to prevent dating and domestic violence against women.

murder victims in the United States between 2003 and 2012, 34 percent were murdered by a male intimate partner while 2.5 percent of male victims were killed by a female intimate partner.

In many cases, battered women feel shame about being the victims of intimate partner violence. Most attacks go unreported. According to the NCADV, only 25 percent of all physical assaults perpetuated by intimate partners are reported to the police.

SEXUAL HARASSMENT

Sexual harassment is persistent, unwelcome behavior of a sexual type that interferes with someone's right to get an education or work at a job. It can include sexual insults or gestures or being touched against one's will. It can include sexual comments on Facebook or in emails or text messages. One type of sexual harassment is called quid pro quo harassment. An example is a male boss who will give a female target a bad review unless she gives in to his sexual advances. Another kind is hostile-environment harassment. This is when an individual persistently makes remarks or advances or touches a woman to the point that she regularly feels uncomfortable and unsafe.

RAPE

Rape is forcing sex upon another person against his or her will. Rape can be committed by a stranger or by someone the victim knows. According to the CDC, about 80 percent of female rape victims were first raped before age twenty-five. The CDC also finds that nearly one in five women have been raped in their lifetimes. However, rape is an underreported crime. According to RAINN, only 344 out of every 1,000 sexual assaults are reported to the police.

SEXUAL ASSAULT AGAINST LGBTQ YOUTH

Sexual violence affects many different people—both male and female, as well as those in the lesbian, gay, bisexual, transgender, and queer (LGBTQ) communities. According to the CDC, LGBTQ youth experience sexual violence at the same or higher rates as heterosexual and cisgender individuals. According to the CDC's National Intimate Partner and Sexual Violence Survey, 44 percent of lesbians and 61 percent of bisexual women experience rape, physical violence, or stalking from an intimate partner, while 26 percent of gay men and 37 percent of bisexual men experience the same. Compare these statistics with 35 percent of heterosexual women and 29 percent of heterosexual men. About half of all transgender individuals will experience sexual violence at some point in their lives.

Because LGBTQ people face greater marginalization and stigma, they are often at a greater risk of sexual violence. Fear of discrimination might also prevent them from seeking help. For those who have been sexually abused, the GLBT National Help Center can be reached at 1-800-246-PRIDE or through their online chat at www.volunteerlogin.org /chat.

One reason why women may not report rapes is that sometimes they are wrongly blamed for them. According to Canada's CBC News, when Michael Sanguinetti, a police officer in Toronto, said, "Women should avoid dressing like sluts in order not to be victimized" in January 2011, many people were furious. In fact, a group of protesters in Toronto marched in what they called a slut walk to protest the comment. Some men in the march even wore dresses to make the point that rape is not the fault of victims, no matter how they dress. Soon similar walks were taking place in countries around the world. Toronto police chief Bill Blair said Sanguinetti's words "place the blame upon victims, and that's not where the blame should ever be placed."

Activists march in a slut walk held on International Women's Day on March 7, 2017. Slut walks evolved to protest comments made by a Toronto police officer that women who dress "like sluts" are more likely to be raped.

HELP END ABUSE

Don't let abusers get away with hurting women. Speak up and take action against all forms of violence against women. Here are some ways to start:

- **Recognize abuse**. It is important to learn some of the signs of relationship abuse in order to recognize it. One sign of an abusive partner is when someone calls repeatedly to check up on where you are. Even if it seems flattering, it is really a form of stalking. If friends are telling you that something doesn't seem right about your romance, listen. If a romantic partner hits you even once, tell a trusted adult immediately. If necessary, press charges or get a restraining order. For more advice or help, call the National Dating Abuse Hotline at (866) 331-9474 or do a live chat on their website (http://www.loveisrespect.org).

- **Return the favor**. The Confidence Coalition has launched an awareness campaign called Friends Say the Tough Stuff...So Say It (http://www.confidencecoalition.org/datingabuseawareness). The campaign encourages friends to speak up when they believe a friend is in an unhealthy relationship. Teens who think a friend is in immediate danger should tell a trusted adult and get help right away.

- **Be safe**. To decrease chances of rape or assault, try

to travel in a group, especially at night. Stand tall and walk confidently. If someone approaches you in a manner that makes you uncomfortable, don't be afraid to back away or run. If someone touches you against your will, yell and make a scene. Do not get into a car with a stranger. If you go to a party, make sure you have a friend who's watching your back. Don't leave your drink unattended— someone could slip something into it. Try to avoid situations where you are alone, especially with someone you don't feel comfortable with.

- **Hold perpetrators accountable**. Join organizations that fight for tougher laws against crimes against women, such as the National Organization for Women (http://www.now.org) or Say NO: UNiTE to End Violence Against Women (http://www.un.org /en/women/endviolence). Teens can also start a petition drive to support laws that end violence.

CHAPTER 5

FIGHTING FOR POLITICAL AND ECONOMIC RIGHTS

When Hillary Clinton became the first female presidential nominee of a major party in US history, she addressed her victory speech to women and girls. "What an incredible honor that you have given me, and I can't believe we just put the biggest crack in that glass ceiling yet," Clinton said. "This is really your victory. This is really your night. And if there are any little girls out there who stayed up late to watch, let me just say I may become the first woman president. But one of you is next." Although Clinton did not end up being elected president of the United States, her nomination was a historic moment. But that doesn't mean that women in the United States and globally don't have a long way to go for equal political and economic rights.

Hillary Clinton made history in 2016 when she became the first ever female presidential nominee of a major party in the United States.

In January 2017, women held just 19.4 percent of the seats in the United States Congress. Women held only 21 of 100 seats in the Senate and 83 out of 535 seats in the House of Representatives. This percentage is so low that, according to data compiled by the Inter-Parliamentary Union, the international organization of parliaments, the United States ranked one hundredth among countries in its number of women lawmakers. Canada ranked sixty-third with 26.3 percent of women lawmakers in its parliament.

WOMEN'S POLITICAL REPRESENTATION GLOBALLY

For women in Canada and the United States, it might be surprising to learn that their countries are not highly ranked in terms of women's political power. The top ten countries for women's representation in politics might be equally surprising. As of 2017, these countries are as follows:

1. Rwanda
2. Bolivia
3. Cuba
4. Iceland
5. Nicaragua
6. Sweden
7. Senegal
8. Mexico
9. South Africa
10. Finland

The countries that offer the least amount of political representation for women include: Kuwait, Lebanon, Papua New Guinea, Haiti, Solomon Islands, Oman, Micronesia, Qatar, Vanuatu, and Yemen. But many North American and European countries have a long way to go, too, to ensure that their female citizens are granted fair and equal political representation in their lawmaking bodies.

Financially, too, women are not yet on equal footing with men. Women make less money, and own less, than men. Many women live lives that are close to the edge. If they get divorced, they are likely to end up much poorer than their husbands. They tend to have less saved for their old age. According to American Community Survey data from 2013, "56.6 of the 45.3 million people living in poverty in the United States are women and girls."

THE PAY GAP

Women are narrowing the gap in many ways professionally, but they are not making the money that men are making, even in the same professions. Women make up less than 5 percent of Fortune 500 CEOs, for instance, according to *Fortune*.

Why? One reason is good old-fashioned sexism. Women generally earn less than men, even for the same work. The American Association of University Women (AAUW) did a study showing that even just one year after graduating from college, women were making less than men. Across all occupations, women earn seventy-seven cents to each dollar that a man earns. Additional explanations for the wage gap include:

- **The "leaky pipeline."** Many women spend time out of the workforce to care for children or disabled or elderly family members. Once they leave their

Professions such as nursing are often called the pink ghetto, meaning that women are more likely to select these careers for flexibility, although they offer lower pay.

jobs, they lose ground in terms of salaries and advancement. It is then very difficult to get a job of equal value to the one that they left—and even harder to get one that would equal the gains they would have made if they had stayed.

- **The "pink ghetto."** The kinds of jobs that women are more likely to select, such as nursing, teaching, or hairdressing, pay less than many traditionally male jobs. Many times, women choose these types of jobs because they allow greater flexibility for raising children.
- **Fear of asking for it**. According to an article on ScienceDaily.com, men are more likely to look for jobs in which competition affects the rate of pay than women are. Also, compared to many young men, women are more likely to avoid negotiating salaries and just to accept the first offer they receive.

VOTING FOR WOMEN'S RIGHTS

Until women have the same representation and the same economic power as men, can they truly have the same rights as men? The votes of young women are more essential than ever. Not only do women need more representation in office, but many laws that positively affect women are at stake and must be fought for.

Because women are more likely to face poverty than men, they rely more on government programs.

For instance, Medicare and Medicaid may face deep cuts in the future. More than half of those who benefit from these programs are women. Medicare is the nation's health insurance program for seniors and disabled younger adults. Medicaid provides health coverage for low-income people, the elderly, people with disabilities, and some families and children. According to the National Women's Law Center, over six in ten elderly individuals who relied on Medicaid were women. It covers millions of mothers and more than one-third of all American children.

The Affordable Care Act (ACA) of 2010 has also been an important step toward health care equality for women. The ACA makes sure that insurance plans cover maternity care and stops health plans from charging women more than men for the same coverage. It requires women's preventive health care services, like breast and cervical cancer screenings, to be covered in health care plans. A repeal of the ACA, as proposed by members of the US government, could have devastating consequences for women.

Even though both men and women receive Social Security, it is a more important source of money for women than it is for men. It is virtually the only source of income for three out of ten women who are sixty-five and older, according to the Social Security Administration. Cuts or reductions could harm these women disproportionately.

Health care legislation such as the Affordable Care Act has helped women receive appropriate medical care. Cuts to these programs could have devastating consequences for women.

MAKE YOUR VOICE HEARD

Important duties of active citizens include staying informed about important issues and sharing your thoughts on how to improve the country with the nation's lawmakers. Voting—and helping other young people to become voters—is a great way to help less well-represented segments of the population to have a voice in the nation's future. Another important topic for young women is learning how the economy works and how they can participate. Teens can make the following worthy efforts in the areas of politics and economics:

- **Get informed.** Start a politics club to pool information. Get a social studies teacher to sponsor the club. Explore how the system works. How does a bill get passed? Who's your congressperson? Not everybody knows this basic information. Vote Smart (http://www.votesmart.org) provides information on how the US government works as well as positions that elected officials or those who are up for election hold.

- **Share your opinion.** Have debates about issues that affect women. Where do you stand? The US Congress makes federal legislative information available to the public on its website (https://www.congress.gov). Here, you can get the text of any bill, as well as the email addresses of all members of Congress. Write to them and let them know what you think. You can also write to the president of the United States to share your opinions. Information about how to contact the president can be found at the White House website (http://www.whitehouse.gov).

- **Get out the vote.** Teens can register to vote if they will be eighteen at the time of the election. But younger teens can also get others involved. Political campaigns and causes always need volunteers. Join phone banks to promote women's causes. Call people to encourage them to come to the polls. If you want to focus on registering young voters, the organization Rock the Vote gives young people the tools to get out the vote (http://rockthevote.com). Organize a voter registration drive, throw a concert with local bands in your town, or hold an issues forum to talk about what matters to young voters in the next election. Rock the Vote alone has already registered millions of young people to vote.

- **Find mentors.** Interview professional women about the kinds of skills and education they needed to become financially successful.
- **Give back.** Help less fortunate women. One example is organizing a dance at a local church or school. Have people pay their entrance fee by making donations of cash or canned goods for a local food bank.

CHAPTER 6

FIGHTING FOR WOMEN GLOBALLY

It may be hard to imagine, but all around the world women and girls continue to die in childbirth every day. According to Maternity Worldwide, 287,000 women die during pregnancy and childbirth each year across the world. That equates to one mother dying every two minutes. Most of these deaths occur in poor and rural areas where girls and women have no access to quality medical care and are unable to receive proper nutrition for themselves and their babies. In cultures where girls get married and have children at young ages, their risk is even greater. Girls and women between the ages of fifteen and twenty are twice as likely to die in childbirth than women in their twenties, while

Women continue to die in pregnancy and childbirth each year across the world because of limited access to quality medical care or an inability to receive proper nutrition.

girls under the age of fifteen are more than five times as likely. For every woman who dies in childbirth, dozens more become injured during labor and delivery. Almost all of these deaths and injuries are preventable.

FISTULA

Huge numbers of women and girls never get any medical attention during their pregnancies or even when they're in labor. Because many are young and often malnourished, sometimes the babies cannot pass through the birth canal correctly. If surgery is not performed in a timely manner, the baby can die in the woman's body and rot her tissue. This can cause a hole called a fistula between the vagina and the bladder or bowels, which causes urine or feces to leak out of the woman uncontrollably. This can cause severe pain and discomfort. If they cannot get surgery to correct the fistula, these women are often exiled to the edges of their villages or left to die. It is estimated that some two million women, predominantly in Africa and the Indian subcontinent, suffer from fistulas. Each year, another fifty thousand to one hundred thousand women are affected, most under age twenty, according to the World Health Organization (WHO).

CHILD BRIDES

According to the United Nations (UN), more than 60 million girls around the world are child brides, married by the age of eighteen. Oftentimes, the girl is taken out of school and away from the protection of her parents. She is married without her consent. She is powerless: she can be beaten not only by her husband but also by his whole family.

One problem some young brides face is dowry death. If the family of the groom is not satisfied with the dowry (or price the bride's family pays the groom), the man's family sometimes murders the girl so that the husband is free to marry a richer bride. According to India's National Crime Records Bureau, 8,233 young women were killed in dowry-related deaths in 2012. Many more deaths might not even be reported.

Another danger child brides face is that their older husbands are more likely to spread sexually transmitted diseases, including HIV/AIDS. In sub-Saharan Africa, 66 percent of the young people (age fifteen to twenty-four) living with HIV are female, according to the UN.

SON PREFERENCE

Nobel Prize–winning economist Amartya Sen drew a lot of attention when he stated that one hundred million girls were missing in 1990. The problem was particularly serious in China and India. What did he mean? Where were the little girls? Sen was referring to the practice called son preference, in which a society's culture leads families to take drastic measures to give birth to or raise only sons, not daughters. Families might do this by terminating pregnancies of girl fetuses or even by killing a female child when she is born. The International Center for Research on Women (ICRW) has reported that the wealth or economic status of families does not reduce son preference, but women's level of education does. According to a major report in the *Economist*, in some

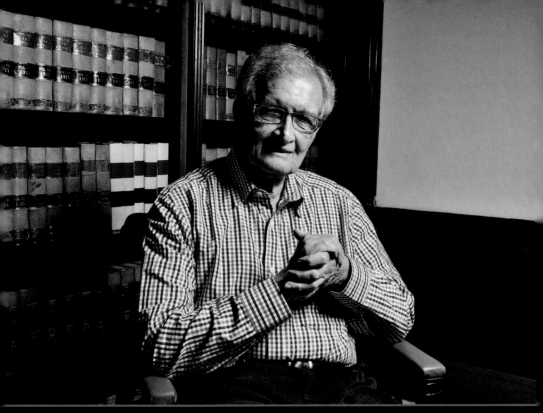

Nobel Prize–winning economist Amartya Sen has been a vocal activist for women's rights and against the practice called son preference.

parts of India and China, 130 boys survive for every 100 girls. Girls who survive in regions that practice female gendercide or son preference often fare less well than their male counterparts. Some girls may get less food and medical care than their brothers and have less educational opportunity.

FEMALE GENITAL MUTILATION (FGM)

In some parts of the world, girls are subjected to an ancient rite of passage by having their genitals cut.

SEX SELECTION

In the Western world, the practice of "sex selection," in which embryos during in vitro fertilization (IVF) are specifically chosen for their sex, is becoming more and more popular. For an extra fee, providers of IVF can use a process known as preimplantation genetic diagnosis (PGD) to determine the sex of an embryo. The parents can then choose which embryos they would like implanted in the mother's uterus. Some doctors and activists have raised ethical concerns about this practice, particularly when it is used to choose one sex predominantly over another. In fact, the Ethics Committee of the American Society of Reproductive Medicine (ASRM) has concluded that sex selection for nonmedical reasons is morally inappropriate. However, the ASRM does recommend PGD when it is used to avoid passing sex-linked genetic disorders from a parent to a child. As more technologies develop that can allow early sex detection or selection, ethicists and women's activists are growing more concerned that male embryos will be chosen or prioritized over female embryos.

This practice is called female circumcision or female genital mutilation (FGM). According to the WHO, approximately two hundred million women and girls alive right now have been subjected to this practice. The process can range from cutting away parts of girls' labia to the most severe form, infibulation. This involves cutting off girls' clitorises, scraping off their labia, and sewing the remaining flesh together. Sometimes the girls' legs are tied together for as many as forty days until the scarred tissue grows together. This brutal practice is often carried out without anesthesia and with crude tools, such as razor blades. In some parts of the world, it would be impossible for a woman who had not had this procedure to get married. There are no health benefits to FGM, and in fact there can be severe health consequences.

WAR CRIMES AGAINST WOMEN

In recent wars in the Democratic Republic of Congo, Sudan, and Iraq, women were raped in shockingly large numbers. The Democratic Republic of Congo, which has experienced unrest since 1996, is a country in which sexual violence against women has been used to devastating effect. In fact, the UN has named the country "the rape capital of the world" and has concluded that up to forty-eight women are raped there every hour. Rape is used as a weapon of war by armed military groups in the country and is used against men and boys as well.

A young Yazidi girl stands inside a displaced persons camp in Iraqi Kurdistan. Yazidi girls and women were kidnapped and raped by ISIS militants as they took over land in Iraq and Syria.

In 1998, the UN made a decision that rape is a crime of genocide because it is committed with the intent to destroy a targeted group. Not only are women damaged by these rapes, they are often rejected by their families, particularly if they become pregnant by their rapists. When the terrorist group the Islamic State of Iraq and Syria (ISIS) took over large amounts of land in Iraq and Syria in 2014, they began a campaign of genocide against the Yazidi religious group native to the area. ISIS members kidnapped Yazidi women and children and forced them into marriages against their will. Rape and sexual violence continue to be used as both a tool of war and genocide by ISIS militants against the Yazidi population in captured territories.

HELPING WOMEN AROUND THE WORLD

Teens can help world efforts to end violence against girls and women and to improve women's health in the developing world. Increasing women's educational and work opportunities is also essential in order for girls to be able to make better lives for themselves, their families, their societies, and each other. The following are important areas in which teens can take action:

- **Signing CEDAW.** In 2000, the UN created a set of Millennial Goals—goals to improve people's lives that they hope to reach by 2015. These solutions address such issues as poverty, education, personal safety, freedom, and work. The UN says that all of the goals include a special focus on women. According to UN Women, "Women perform 66 percent of the world's work, produce 50 percent of the food, but earn 10 percent of the income and own one percent of the property."

One source of potential protection for women is a UN convention called the Convention to Eliminate All Forms of Discrimination Against Women (CEDAW). This international agreement affirms human rights and equality for women around the world. It defines what discrimination against women is, and it sets an agenda for actions to end it. Many countries around the world have ratified this treaty, but the United States has not. To help, teens in the United States can contact their senators with a petition or organize a letter-writing campaign to urge the government to sign the treaty. For more information and other ways to help, see the Feminist Majority Foundation website (http://www.feminist.org/global/cedaw.html).

- **Women's health—a human right.** Organizations such as the UN are now looking at safe childbirth from a human rights perspective. Economist Amartya Sen has said that governments should measure their success not just by their gross domestic product but by measuring human development: Are its citizens meeting at least a minimum standard of well-being in their lives? One form of well-being that the UN and other organizations propose is a right to safe childbirth. The tiny percentage of maternal deaths in the developed world proves that childbirth does not have to be the major killer it is in countries such as Afghanistan, where one out of eleven women die giving birth. Young people in the United States can help by pairing with charities such as WomenDeliver .org and Care.org to raise money and to spread the word through their social media and web pages. They can also write to their senators and representatives to ask for more foreign aid to be used to solve this problem.

- **Female genital mutilation.** Charities are working in a number of sub-Saharan African nations to address the problem of female genital mutilation. The organization ActionAid (http://actionaidusa .org) started a project in Woliso, Ethiopia, in 1998. They learned that "changing social attitudes, rather than passing laws against the practice, was key." They began to spread the word that FGM is related to the spread of AIDS. Tostan (http://www.tostan.org) works to end FGM in Senegal. Tostan, which means "breakthrough" in Senegal's major language, created African-style education programs to talk about the dangers of FGM. It has gotten support from more than five thousand villages in the country. Check out its website for ways to help.

- **Education.** Another problem that many girls face is lack of education. Education helps to give girls a wider perspective on the world. It gives them power and dignity. It gives them skills they can teach their children. And it gives them the chance to get decent work so they can participate fully in society. Unfortunately, according to UNICEF, fifty-nine million children around the world are out of school—and the majority of them are girls. For example, in sub-Saharan Africa only two out of thirty-five countries have reached gender parity in the percentage of girls and boys who attend school. In South and West Asia, 80 percent of girls are unlikely ever to attend school as compared to 16 percent of boys.

Some organizations that support girls' education include the Afghan Institute of Learning (http://www.afghaninstituteoflearning .org) and the Campaign for Female Education, or Camfed (http://camfed.org). Camfed supports education in Africa and lets people set up personal fundraising pages. The organization suggests ways to encourage others to donate to your page—for example, hosting a movie screening of the Camfed movie (available for a small cost) or asking for donations instead of presents on your birthday. Even just signing up for their mailing list earns a girl in Africa a year of pencils. According to Camfed's website, "When you educate a girl in Africa, everything changes. She'll be three times less likely to get HIV/AIDS, earn 25 percent more income and have a smaller, healthier family."

- **Helping women work.** In 2006, Mohammed Yunus won a Nobel Prize for developing a system of microloans—a practice that focuses largely on women. He found that instead of giving charity for large-scale projects, giving tiny loans to people to start their own businesses was a very effective way to lift women out of poverty. For example, if you lend money to a woman to start her own business, she can take care of her family and gain economic power. Studies have shown that when women in the developing world earn money, the benefit to their families is larger than when it is given to men. Now a number of organizations focus on microloans in the developing world. One excellent site for microlending is Kiva (http://www.kiva .org). For $25, you can choose the exact person you want to lend money to—and you will even get that money back. One example is a forty-nine-year-old farmer, Vastina, who borrowed $450 to harvest corn and work on her small banana plantation in Uganda. She hopes to buy more land so she can grow more crops and earn money to educate her six children.

  The organization Women for Women (http:// www.womenforwomen.org) trains women to gain valuable work skills in the developing world. According to the organization's website, Azada is one Afghan girl they helped. She was fourteen when she

Activist and Women for Women International founder
Zainab Salbi speaks at the foundation's annual awards gala.

was married to a cousin. She had two children with
him, but he abused her so much that her father let her
divorce. She entered a Women for Women program
that taught her to cut semiprecious stones for making
jewelry. Now she teaches gem cutting to other women.
Azada says, "I never thought that I would have the
opportunity to support myself without a man. Now ...
I am doing it."

CHAPTER 7

STARTING AT HOME

While women and girls face many challenges globally in regions plagued with famine and war, many also face challenges in their homes or at their schools. Sometimes, these challenges seem insurmountable and they take drastic—and irreversible—steps. In November 2016, eighteen-year-old Brandy Vela felt hopeless. She had been bullied for her weight both online and in school. Several months earlier, Vela's tormentors had begun making fake Facebook pages and using untraceable apps to harass her day and night. It became too much for Vela to take. On November 29, Vela shot herself to death at home in front of her family. They had tried to save her after receiving a text from her apologizing for what she was going to do.

Working as an activist for women and girls can begin right at home by combating bullying when you see it occurring.

RELATIONAL AGGRESSION

When many people think of bullying, they think of hitting, punching, and kicking. Studies prove that girls bully just as much as boys but often in a different way. Bullying by girls tends to be of a type called relational aggression. This means engaging in actions that manipulate relationships in order to hurt another person. Some examples include hostile body language, like glaring, eye-rolling, or spreading gossip; using demeaning language; excluding others; lying to or misleading someone; or cyberbullying. A girl engaging in relational aggression might suddenly turn on a friend for no apparent reason. She might reveal her secrets. Or she might refer to another girl with derogatory words.

Why do girls sometimes act this way? Girls are expected to be sweet. When girls act angry, they are often accused of being unfeminine. This can make girls more indirect than boys in the way they express their anger. So, for instance, if one girl is mad at another for telling a joke she thinks is mean, she might not say, "Cut it out," and move on. She might fake niceness to the friend's face and then reveal one of the friend's secrets behind her back.

Being indirect can be useful and effective at times. But there are problems with it. You can add more tools to your communication toolbox. Learning to be assertive—to express your thoughts openly but without abusing others' rights—can help you to keep friendships you might otherwise lose.

Teens who are being bullied and can't get the bullies to stop should speak to a trusted teacher or administrator at school. Putting up with bullying behavior is harmful for both the bullied individual and the bully. If you see bullying, report it to an adult or distract the bully. To avoid cyberabuse, change your passwords regularly, and if the abuse continues, call customer support, block or delete the bullies, or call the police.

THE GIFTS OF FRIENDSHIP

Girls are often capable of extraordinary compassion and true and deep friendship. What gifts do girls bring to friendships with others? They are more verbal at an earlier age. They are often very aware emotionally. Female friendships can be a powerful force. They can be one of the great joys of life. Some of the signs of a good friendship are watching each other's backs, sympathizing when a friend is sad, celebrating victories, and telling the truth—gently. Friends can teach each other how to work together toward goals, to play fair, and to connect to others in a positive way.

Female friendship can be extremely rewarding and a real source of joy in one's life.

Another part of being a good friend is helping a friend if she is in danger of harming herself by doing such things as cutting, suicide, or taking drugs. Get help for your friend—even if she doesn't want you to. If a friend is in danger of hurting herself, you may need to call 911 or a crisis line.

1. How can I get help if I am being bullied?

2. How can I help a friend I know is being bullied?

3. What responsibilities does the school have in stopping bullying?

4. How should I handle a conflict with someone in my social circle?

5. How do I help a friend who has told me a worrisome secret about her relationship or about her physical or mental health?

6. What should I do if someone I know is being stalked, harassed, or abused?

7. What steps can I take to start a club for girls' and women's rights?

8. What steps can I take to get a school group involved in community volunteering?

9. How can I start a girls' sports team in school?

10. How can I get permission to use public spaces in the school, such as the school auditorium or library, to promote girls' and women's rights?

EVOLVING FRIENDSHIPS

Sometimes, friends' interests may change. Be willing to let go of a friendship that isn't working for you. If you think there's a chance of saving the friendship, tell your friend specifically why you are feeling concerned or hurt. If you can't work it out, remain civil and move on. Then do something physical or join a new activity with your newfound free time.

You should also make an effort to make new friends. Don't just look in the obvious places. Join clubs, volunteer, and do activities with people who are interested in the same things you are. Break out of your comfort zone to speak with a potential new friend. It can feel awkward to invite someone you don't know well to do something with you. But if you take a chance, you might just make a great new friend.

Finally, be a good friend to yourself. Take care of you. Some days just stink, even if your life is good. If you're looking for ways to bring cheer to your day, they can include laughing, napping, dancing, playing, hugging, and expressing gratitude. You can put inspirational quotes on Post-it notes and put them where you will see them.

Another thing you can do is practice positive body language. Walk tall. Give yourself credit when you reach a goal.

In addition to cultivating friendships, teens should also learn to become good friends to themselves.

ACTIVISM AT HOME

Activism on behalf of women can start at home. Teens can use their voices and minds to stand up for themselves and those around them. A good place to start is with the following acts of caring and courage:

- **Be kind to yourself.** Dr. Kristin Neff, a professor of human development and culture, wrote the book *Self-Compassion: Stop Beating Yourself Up and Leave Insecurity Behind.* "With self-compassion, if you care about yourself, you do what's healthy for you rather than what's harmful to you," she says. She recommends "compassion breaks," which involve repeating mantras like, "I'm going to be kind to myself in this moment." Do you treat

A good way for teens to value women's contributions right at home is by taking the time to listen to the wisdom older women in their lives can offer them.

yourself as well as you treat your friends? Think about it, and try to make sure you do.

- **Stop hurtful words.** Organize and participate in awareness-raising projects like National No Name-Calling Week (https://www.glsen.org/nonamecallingweek). Its website has activities for students, teachers, and schools.

- **Cross the generations.** Teens should reach out to different generations, such as sharing wisdom and skills with younger girls or taking the time to listen to the older women in their lives. They may end up being a valuable resource as well.

- **Build your own competence.** Pay attention, be serious, and follow through. Develop your talents. Be daring. Keep trying. Try to live the life you want. The actions you take today are training you to be the adult you will become. A stone embedded in a building in sufragette Alice Paul's alma mater, Swarthmore College, says, "Use well thy freedom." Use the freedom you have been given (through the efforts of others) to live the best, healthiest, most empowering life you can live. It's worth it.

GLOSSARY

ABOLITIONIST One who opposes, or wants to abolish, slavery.

AIRBRUSH To use photographic or computer-based techniques to change photos.

ANOREXIA A serious disorder in which an abnormal fear of being fat leads to restricted eating, malnutrition, and excessive weight loss.

ASSAULT Attack.

CEO Chief executive officer, or the head of a company.

CISGENDER Describes people whose sense of gender identity corresponds with the sex they were assigned at birth.

EMBRYO A human or animal in the early stages of development, typically from the second to eighth week after the fertilization of an egg by a sperm.

ENTREPRENEURSHIP The setting up of one's own business.

FISTULA A dangerous condition in which there is an opening between a woman's birth canal and rectum or bladder.

GENDERCIDE The systematic elimination of offspring because of their gender, through sex-selection abortions or killing of newborns.

HEMORRHAGE Rapid, heavy bleeding.

HIV/AIDS A life-threatening illness caused by a virus, often spread through sex.

HUMAN PAPILLOMAVIRUS (HPV) A virus that

can cause cervical and other kinds of cancer,
usually spread through sexual contact.

LIBIDO Sex drive.

METABOLIC SYNDROME A destructive health
condition that includes diabetes, heart
disease, and high blood pressure, often
caused by obesity.

PERPETRATOR A person who carries out a crime.

PINK GHETTO A term used to describe the types
of jobs that are considered typical "women's
jobs," such as nursing and teaching.

RAPE When one person forces sex activity, often
sexual intercourse, upon another person
without their consent.

SEXISM The unjust treatment of one gender
against another.

STALKING A pattern of repetitive behaviors
in which one person spies, threatens, keeps
trying to communicate with, and possibly
damages the property of a victim who does
not want those attentions.

STEREOTYPE An exaggerated, frequently unfair
image or idea about a certain group.

SUFFRAGE The right to vote.

TRANSGENDER Describes people whose sense of
gender identity does not correspond with the
sex they were assigned at birth.

Centers for Disease Control and Prevention (CDC)
Division of Adolescent and School Health (DASH)
    4770 Buford Highway NE
    MS K29
    Atlanta, GA 30341
(800) CDC-INFO [232-4636]
Website: www.cdc.gov/healthyyouth
Twitter: @CDC_DASH
This government resource provides extensive
    information about aspects of young people's
    health, including nutrition, violence, sexuality,
    and more. It gives statistical information as
    well as information on how girls can live
    healthier lives.

Feminist Majority Foundation
    1600 Wilson Boulevard, Suite 801
    Arlington, VA 22209
(703) 522-2214
Website: www.feminist.org
Facebook: @FeministMajorityFoundation
Twitter: @MajoritySpeaks
This international organization fights for equality
    for women, particularly through violence
    prevention and advancing women's economic
    opportunities. It offers news about women,
    ways girls can take action, a career center,
    and more.

MediaSmarts
205 Catherine Street, Suite 100
Ottawa, ON K2P 1C3
Canada
(613) 224-7721
Email: info@mediasmarts.ca
Website: www.mediasmarts.ca
Facebook: @MediaSmarts
Twitter: @MediaSmarts
MediaSmarts focuses its efforts on equipping
adults with media and digital literacy skills.
The organization features articles that explain
the effects of media on girls and women.

National Organization for Women (NOW)
1100 H Street NW, Suite 300
Washington, DC 20005
(202) 628-8NOW [8669]
Website: www.now.org
Facebook: @NationalNOW
Twitter: @NationalNOW
NOW is a prominent organization that works
for the betterment of women. NOW offers
internships, campus activities, and task
force membership for young people who
are interested in women's rights. Its website
includes news, projects, action steps, and other
useful information.

Status of Women Canada
 22 Eddy Street, 10th Floor
 Gatineau, QC J8X 2V6
 Canada
(613) 995-7835
Website: www.swc-cfc.gc.ca
Facebook: @womencanada
Twitter: @Women_Canada
This federal government organization in Canada
 promotes women's equality. It encourages
 women's leadership, works to end violence
 against women, and supports other important
 goals. Its website provides useful information
 on women's status in Canada.

UN Women
 220 East 42nd Street
 New York, NY 10017
(646) 781-4400
Website: www.unwomen.org
Facebook: @unwomen
Twitter: @UN_Women
UN Women is a United Nations entity that works
 for the empowerment of women and the
 elimination of discrimination against women
 and girls. It is a clearinghouse for important
 information about women of the world and
 the efforts being made to help them. The

website includes links about how individuals can help as well.

WEBSITES

Due to the changing nature of internet links, Rosen Publishing has developed an online list of websites related to the subject of this book. This site is updated regularly. Please use this link to access the list:

http://www.rosenlinks.com/WITW/Activist

Abouraya, Karen Leggett and L. C. Wheatley. *Malala Yousafzai: Warrior With Words.* Great Neck, NY: StarWalk Kids Media, 2014.

Hoffman, Mary. *Daughters of Time.* Dorking, UK: Templar Publishing, 2014.

Lauricella, Leanne. *Goats of Anarchy: One Woman's Quest to Save the World One Goat at a Time.* Lexington, KY: Rock Point, 2017.

Levinson, Cynthia and Vanessa Brantley Newton. *The Younger Marcher: The Story of Audrey Faye Hendricks, a Young Civil Rights Activist.* New York, NY: Atheneum Books for Young Readers, 2017.

Levy, Debbie and Elizabeth Baddeley. *I Dissent: Ruth Bader Ginsburg Makes Her Mark.* New York, NY: Simon & Schuster Books for Young Readers, 2016.

Nardo, Don. *The Split History of the Women's Suffrage Movement: A Perspectives Flip Book.* North Mankato, MN: Compass Point Books, 2014.

Schatz, Kate and Miriam Klein Stahl. *Rad American Women A–Z: Rebels, Trailblazers, and Visionaries Who Shaped Our History...and Our Future!* San Francisco, CA: City Lights Publishers, 2015.

Shetterly, Margot Lee. *Hidden Figures*
(Young Readers Edition). New York, NY:
HarperCollins, 2016.

Spence, Kelly. *Malala Yousafzai: Defender of
Education for Girls*. St. Catherines, Ontario:
Crabtree Publishing Company, 2017.

Stone, Tanya Lee. *Girl Rising: Changing the World
One Girl at a Time*. New York, NY: Wendy
Lamb Books, 2017.

Thomas, Angie. *The Hate U Give*. New York, NY:
Balzer + Bray, 2017.

Yousafzai, Malala and Patricia McCormick. *I Am
Malala: How One Girl Stood Up for Education
and Changed the World* (Young Readers
Edition). New York, NY: Little, Brown Books
for Young Readers, 2016.

American Psychological Association, Task Force on the Sexualization of Girls. *Report of the APA Task Force on the Sexualization of Girls.* 2010. http://www.apa.org/pi/women /programs/girls/report-full.pdf.

Bennett, Jessica, and Jesse Ellison. "Women Will Rule the World." *Newsweek,* July 5, 2010. http://www.thedailybeast.com /newsweek/2010/07/06/women-will-rule -the-world.html.

Blumberg, Joseph. "Virtual Reality: Dartmouth Researchers Challenge Photo Retouching with Rating System." *Dartmouth Now,* November 28, 2011. http://now.dartmouth.edu/2011/11 /virtual-reality-dartmouth-researcher s-challenge-photo-retouching-with -rating-system.

Bureau of Justice Statistics. "Intimate Partner Violence." November 21, 2013. https://www .bjs.gov/index.cfm?ty=pbdetail&iid=4801.

Catalano, Shannan, Michael R. Rand, Erica L. Smith, and Howard Snyder. "Female Victims of Violence." Bureau of Justice Statistics, September 30, 2009. http://bjs.ojp.usdoj.gov /index.cfm?ty=pbdetail&iid=2020.

CBC News. "Toronto 'Slut Walk' Takes to City Streets." April 3, 2011. http://www.cbc.ca /news/canada/toronto/story/2011/04/03 /slut-walk-toronto.html.

Centers for Disease Control and Prevention. "CDC
– Sexual Behaviors – Adolescent and School
Health." March 10, 2017. http://www.cdc.gov
/HealthyYouth/sexualbehaviors/index.htm.

Centers for Disease Control and Prevention.
"Childhood Obesity Facts: Prevalence of
Childhood Obesity in the United States, 2011
–2014." December 22, 2016. https://www.cdc
.gov/obesity/data/childhood.html.

Centers for Disease Control and Prevention.
"Press Release: Sexual Violence, Stalking, and
Intimate Partner Violence Widespread in the
US." December 14, 2011. http://www.cdc.gov
/media/releases/2011/p1214_sexual
_violence.html.

Dessen, Sarah. Dreamland. New York, NY:
Viking, 2000.

Diegnan, Michael. "Where Are They Now?
Julie Krone." ABC Sports Online, April 19,
2001. http://www.espn.go.com
/abcsports/s/2001/0417/1174371.html.

Economist. "The War on Baby Girls: Gendercide."
March 4, 2010. http://www.economist.com
/node/15606229.

Grimké, Sarah M. Letters on the Equality and the
Condition of Woman. Boston, MA:
I. Knapp, 1838. http://openlibrary.org/books
/OL7005544M/Letters_on_the_equality_of
_the_sexes_and_the_condition_of_woman.

Hanson-Harding, Alexandra. *Great American Speeches.* New York, NY: Scholastic Professional Books, 1997.

Inter-Parliamentary Union (IPU). "Women in Parliaments: World Classification." March 1, 2017. http://www.ipu.org/wmn-e/classif.htm.

Keating, Caitlin. "Teen's Family Reveals the Intense Bullying Before Her Suicide in Front of Them: 'It Was Stalking.'" *People,* December 14, 2016. http://people.com/crime /cyberbullied-teen-brandy-vela-family.

Kristof, Nicholas D., and Sheryl WuDunn. *Half the Sky: Turning Oppression into Opportunity for Women Worldwide.* New York, NY: Alfred A. Knopf, 2009.

Lake Tanganyika Floating Health Clinic. "About." Retrieved April 3, 2017. http://floatingclinic .org/about.

Masters, Kim. "Why the Odds Are Still Stacked Against Women in Hollywood." *Hollywood Reporter,* December 9, 2011. http://www .hollywoodreporter.com/news/angelina -jolie-kristen-stewart-emma-watson -katheryn-bigelow-269694.

"Modern History Sourcebook: Sojourner Truth: 'Ain't I a Woman?', December 1851." Fordham University. Retrieved April 3, 2017. https:// sourcebooks.fordham.edu/mod/sojtruth -woman.asp.

National Association of Anorexia Nervosa and Associated Disorders (ANAD). "Eating Disorders Statistics." Retrieved April 3, 2017. http://www.anad.org/get-information/about-eating-disorders/eating-disorders-statistics.

National Coalition Against Domestic Violence. "Domestic Violence Facts." Retrieved April 3, 2017. http://www.ncadv.org/files/DomesticViolenceFactSheet(National).pdf.

Nobelprize.org. "The Nobel Peace Prize 2011 – Press Release." October 7, 2011. http://www.nobelprize.org/nobel_prizes/peace/laureates/2011/press.html.

United Nations Population Fund (UNFPA). "HIV/AIDS." Retrieved April 3, 2017. http://www.unfpa.org/hiv-aids.

United Nations Secretary-General's Campaign: Unite to End Violence Against Women. "Fact Sheet." United Nations Department of Public Information, DPI/2498. Retrieved April 3, 2017. http://www.un.org/en/women/endviolence/pdf/VAW.pdf.

University of Chicago. "Women Less Interested Than Men in Jobs Where Individual Competition Determines Wages." *ScienceDaily*, January 13, 2011. http://www.sciencedaily.com/releases/2011/01/110113131438.htm.

UN Women. "Fast Facts: Statistics on Violence Against Women and Girls." Retrieved April 3,

2017. http://www.endvawnow.org/en
/articles/299-fast-facts-statistics-on-violence
-against-women-and-girls-.html.

US Department of Health and Human Services. "Physical Activity Guidelines for Americans." Retrieved April 3, 2017. https://health.gov /paguidelines/guidelines.

Ward, Geoffrey C., Martha Saxton, Ann D. Gordon, and Ellen Carol DuBois. *Not For Ourselves Alone: The Story of Elizabeth Cady Stanton and Susan B. Anthony: An Illustrated History*. New York, NY: Alfred A. Knopf, 1999.

World Health Organization. "Female Genital Mutilation." February 2017. http://www.who .int/mediacentre/factsheets/fs241/en.

World Health Organization. "10 Facts on Obstetric Fistula." May 2014. http://www.who .int/features/factfiles/obstetric_fistula/en.

Young, Katie. "Kate Winslet and the Celebrities Wiping Out Airbrushing." *Telegraph*, October 22, 2015. http://www.telegraph.co .uk/beauty/people/Kate-Winslet -bans-airbrushing.

ABOUT THE AUTHORS

Lena Koya is a writer and scholar based in Long Island, New York. She cares very much about women's issues and works to raise her two young sons as feminists.

Alexandra Hanson-Harding has been scribbling away since she started her first journal at age fourteen. Now she's written more than 130 journals! She has also had a long career writing professionally and is the author of fifteen books and more than one hundred articles for young people. She has written about everything from the lives of the First Ladies to the early women workers' struggle called the Waistmakers' Revolt of 1909. Alexandra lives in New Jersey with her husband, Brian, and has two sons—good men who also care about women's rights.

PHOTO CREDITS

Design & Layout: Nicole Russo-Duca; Editor & Photo Research: Elizabeth Schmermund.